"A
"ALL THE STARS

Primo Scagnetti

**HELLO
CARLO
PRESS**

SZA:
"A" is for
"ALL THE STARS"

INTRODUCTION

Solána Imani Rowe gave herself the stage name SZA (influenced by RZA of the Wu Tang Clan). She has released two studio albums, the first in 2017, and the second in 2022. These were preceded by 3 EPs released in 2012, 2013, and 2014 respectively.

She has collaborated with numerous artists, including Kendrick Lamar, Doja Cat, Chance the Rapper, Travis Scott, Phoebe Bridgers, and Ty Dolla $ign, to name a few. She is a Golden Globe and Academy Award nominee due to her collaboration with Kendrick Lamar on "All the Stars" from *the BLACK PANTHER* (2018) soundtrack.

This project simply pairs the alphabet with 26 corresponding songs from her studio albums, her most recent EP, and a soundtrack appearance.

- P.S., March 2023

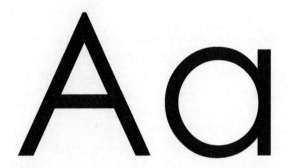

is for

"**A**LL THE
ST**A**RS"
(Kendrick Lamar, SZA)

FROM THE
SOUNDTRACK
ALBUM:

*BLACK
PANTHER:
THE ALBUM*
(2018)

Bb

is for
"BABYLON"
(featuring Kendrick Lamar)

FROM THE EP:

Z

(2014)

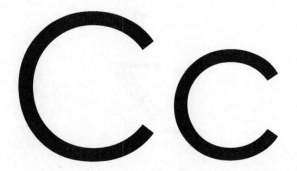

is for

"**C**ONCEITED"

FROM THE STUDIO ALBUM:

SOS

(2022)

Dd

is for
"**D**REW
BARRYMORE"

FROM THE STUDIO ALBUM:

CTRL

(2017)

Ee

is for
"s**EE**k &
d**E**stroy"

FROM THE STUDIO ALBUM:

SOS

(2022)

Ff

is for

"**F**AR"

FROM THE STUDIO ALBUM:

SOS
(2022)

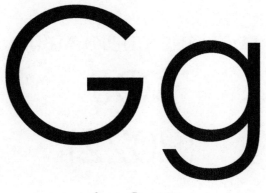

is for

"**G**HOST IN THE MACHINE"

(featuring Phoebe Bridgers)

FROM THE STUDIO ALBUM:

SOS
(2022)

Hh

is for

"**H**IIIJACK"

FROM THE EP:

Z

(2014)

Ii

is for

"I HATE YOU"

FROM THE STUDIO ALBUM:

SOS
(2022)

is for
"JULIA"

FROM THE EP:

Z

(2014)

Kk

is for
"KILL BILL"

FROM THE STUDIO ALBUM:

SOS

(2022)

LI

is for
"**L**OVE
GA**L**ORE"
(featuring Travis Scott)

FROM THE STUDIO ALBUM:
CTRL
(2017)

is for
"**M**ILES"

FROM THE STUDIO ALBUM:

CTRL

(2017)

(DELUXE VERSION)

Nn

is for
"NOBODY
GETS ME"

FROM THE STUDIO ALBUM:

SOS
(2022)

.

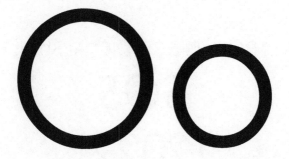

is for
"OPEN ARMS"
(featuring Travis Scott)

FROM THE STUDIO ALBUM:

SOS
(2022)

Pp

is for
"PROM**"**

FROM THE STUDIO ALBUM:
CTRL
(2017)

is for

"..*q*uite like..."

FROM THE SONG:
"LOVE LANGUAGE"

FROM THE STUDIO ALBUM:
SOS
(2022)

Rr

is for

"SHATTERED
RING"

FROM THE EP:

Z

(2014)

Ss

is for
"**S**UPERMODEL"

FROM THE STUDIO ALBUM:

CTRL

(2017)

Tt

is for

"2AM"
("TWO AM")

FROM THE STUDIO ALBUM:

CTRL

(2017)

(DELUXE VERSION)

Uu

is for
"**U**SED"

(featuring Don Toliver)

FROM THE STUDIO ALBUM:

SOS
(2022)

is for
"do**V**ES IN THE WIND"
(featuring Kendrick Lamar)

FROM THE STUDIO ALBUM:
CTRL
(2017)

is for

"THE
WEEKEND"

FROM THE STUDIO ALBUM:

CTRL
(2017)

is for
"SMOKING ON MY
e**X** PACK"

FROM THE STUDIO ALBUM:

SOS
(2022)

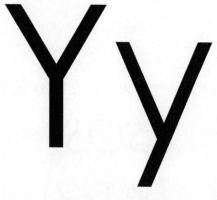

is for

"CHILDS

PLA**y**"

(featuring Chance the Rapper)

FROM THE EP:

Z

(2014)

Zz

is for

"SNOOZE"

FROM THE STUDIO ALBUM:

SOS
(2022)

STUDIO ALBUM
DISCOGRAPHY
(2017 - 2022)

CTRL
JUN 2017

SOS
DEC 2022

(featuring Mac Miller)

(featuring The Weeknd)

JAY-Z + KANYE WEST
WATCH THE THRONE TOUR
(A CHRONOLOGY)

JUSTIN BIEBER vs. DRAKE vs.
The WEEKND
THE ALBUMS (2010-2022)

21 SAVAGE vs. DRAKE vs.
TY DOLLA $IGN
THE ALBUMS (2010-2022)

J. COLE vs. TY DOLLA $IGN vs.
TRAVIS SCOTT
THE ALBUMS (2011-2022)

And much, much more
coming soon.

Say hello at:
twitter.com/primoscagnetti
@PrimoScagnetti